# AMERICAN CRAFTS

## EASY-TO-MAKE PROJECTS FROM
## TRADITIONAL FOLK CRAFTS

### MADELINE H. GUYON

NATIONAL GALLERY OF ART, WASHINGTON

To My Parents

First published in the United States of America in 1992 by
RIZZOLI INTERNATIONAL PUBLICATIONS, INC.
300 Park Avenue South, New York, New York 10010

Introduction copyright © 1992 National Gallery of Art, Washington, D.C.
Index of American Design Illustrations copyright © 1992 National Gallery of Art,
Washington, D.C.
Text and Projects copyright © 1992 Madeline Guyon
Photographs of Projects copyright © 1992 Rizzoli International Publications, Inc.

Library of Congress Cataloging in Publication Data

Guyon, Madeline H.
American Crafts : easy-to-make projects from traditional folk crafts / Madeline H. Guyon.
p.  cm.
ISBN 0-8478-1579-X
1. Handicraft—United States.  2. Folk art—United States.
I. National Gallery of Art (U.S.) II.  Title.
TT23.G88  1992     92-4789
680'.973—dc20     CIP

Design by Gilda Hannah
Photography of Projects by George Ross
Printed and bound in Singapore

# CONTENTS

# INTRODUCTION

The Index of American Design is a collection of approximately 17,000 watercolors by more than 1,000 artists. They depict American decorative arts from the colonial period through the nineteenth century. Established during the Depression as a federal work project to employ commercial artists, the Index was active from 1935 to 1942 in thirty-four states and the District of Columbia. Reflecting a growing interest in folk art during the 1930s, Index artists produced renderings of ceramics, costume, furniture, glass, carvings, tools, textiles, and domestic utensils. These were meant to provide students, scholars, collectors, artists, manufacturers, and designers with exemplary models of American design. Various watercolor techniques were employed by Index artists to record objects meticulously with exact fidelity to nature. As a result, many of the renderings are extraordinary examples of *trompe l'oeil* painting, reproducing color, texture, and detail to a remarkable degree.

Published portfolios of the finest renderings were the Index's ultimate goal. Unfortunately, America's entrance into World War II and the termination of many federal work programs brought the Index of American Design to a premature close with the portfolios left unpublished. The National Gallery of Art became the permanent home of the Index of American Design in 1943. The Index is open by appointment to interested students, scholars, and collectors.

# NOTE TO THE READER

All of the projects in this book are inspired by crafts and design motifs from the Index of American Design, a collection housed at the National Gallery of Art. Each project is made from inexpensive, easily obtainable materials, some of which you already may have at home. Places to buy materials include sewing centers, crafts stores, art supply stores, stationery stores, and variety stores.

While directions are easy to understand, parents are encouraged to take an active role in supervising and assisting young people in making these projects, especially those that require the use of sharp tools. Keep in mind that creativity and expression are more important than a perfectly finished project.

You can make copies of the project patterns on a photocopier or by using tracing paper. Work in good light and on a protected work surface. When tired, put work aside and begin again the next day. Always clean tools at the end of the day.

Have fun and remember that many of the original pieces illustrated in this book were made by people with little formal art training. We hope that both parents and children will not only enjoy making the projects, but also discover a little about the history of the items so wonderfully rendered in the watercolors from the Index of American Design.

I am honored to work with and I thank my editor, Lois Brown, and at the National Gallery of Art, Ysabel Lightner and Frances Smyth.

Thank you also to the Index of American Design curators, Carlotta Owens and Charlie Richie, who early on gave me time to pore through all 17,000 microfiche images and allowed me to view a few originals.

Many thanks to George Ross for superb project photographs, to Gilda Hannah for her talented book design, and to Isabelle Bleecker for her diligence.

A special thank you to Mum for her ideas, support, and suggestions, and to my sister Roberta and family for supply outings. Thanks also to Dory Ryan·for my home away from home, Stewart & Sandy Thomson for advice and friendship, Carol Sanders and especially Christy Austin for getting my graphic arts up to speed, and to Nanette Wiser at Copley News Service for never complaining about my increasingly late columns.

Most of all my love and thanks go to my husband, Bill Morrow, for being my biggest supporter and encouraging me to keep going.

MADELINE H. GUYON

*Hooked Rug,
1780*

## HOOKED RUG

Early settlers coming to America brought many skills, including rug making, but the hooked rug is an American development originating in New England. This method of drawing loops (scraps, strings, and bits of wool and yarn) through a backing material was taken to Europe and used by the French, English, Welsh, and Scots.

Making a hooked rug is not difficult, but it does require both the ability to make artistic choices and manual dexterity. Many early examples are based on geometric or abstract designs and look as modern as products of the studios and workshops of today's avant-garde artists.

Florals were the most popular motifs; other popular designs featured leaves and homely themes such as a favorite pet, farm animals, trees, and houses.

## *Project:* HOOKED RUG

You can work on this rug with a friend, sitting side by side. When you are done you can display the rug at the side of your bed, on a chair, or on the wall, like a picture.

Making a latch-hook rug is simple and quick to do; it's like coloring a picture with bits of yarn. Practice first on a small piece of canvas and use it as a dollhouse rug.

You can follow the design in this book or make up one of your own. To make your own, take a piece of paper the size you want your rug to be and draw a simple picture on it. The directions explain how to mark our design or yours onto the canvas and how to use the latch hook to "knot" the precut yarn.

### Materials

- rug canvas (A piece 14" x 15" allows a 4" border for the hem around our design. If you are using your own design, use a piece of canvas 4" bigger in each direction than your pattern.)
- masking tape
- permanent marking pen
- latch hook
- precut rug yarn: 2 packs brown, 1 pack each other color shown on key, or colors for your design
- pins
- heavy-duty sewing thread
- large-eyed needle
- scissors

**To Prepare the Canvas**

1. Bind all the edges of the canvas with the masking tape to keep them from unraveling while you are working.

2. To establish the lower left corner of the design, hold the canvas horizontally (with the wider dimension going from left to right). At the bottom left corner, measure 2" in from the side and bottom edges, and make a small mark with the pen at the intersection of the mesh threads at this point.

*Note:* Using a permanent marking pen ensures that the marks will never run and spoil your work.

**To Mark the Design on the Canvas**

*Note:* For our design, each square on the chart is equal to one mesh (the horizontal thread between two vertical threads on the canvas) and represents one knotted piece of yarn.

1. Refer to the chart and count the squares along the bottom row of the design. Starting at the mark on the canvas, count off and mark across the same number of horizontal mesh threads. Be sure to follow the same horizontal thread across the canvas. The last marked mesh will be the lower-right corner of the design.

2. In the same way, mark the side edges by referring to the chart, counting and marking the horizontal mesh threads up from the bottom corners.

3. Mark the horizontal mesh threads at the top of the design to complete the fourth side.

4. Count the squares on the chart for the stripes and outline the corresponding mesh threads on the canvas.

5. Outline the cat in the same way, adding marks for eyes, mouth, and stripes.

*For Your Own Design*

1. Lightly tape your drawing to the worktable. Place the canvas on top of it, centering it over your design. Tape the canvas to the paper or work surface in one or two places to keep it from moving.

2. Using the pen, mark the outline of the design onto the horizontal mesh threads of the canvas.

3. Remove the canvas and bind all its edges with masking tape.

**To Use the Latch Hook**

1. Hold the handle of the latch hook in your right hand. Left-handers should follow instructions using their left hand and complete the rug from bottom to top, row by row, the same as right-handers.

2. With your other hand, fold one piece of yarn in half around the stem of the hook, below the swinging latch. Hold the ends of the yarn between your fingers as you do the next step (diagram 1).

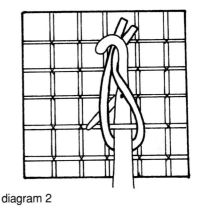

diagram 1

3. Insert the hook into the canvas, under one horizontal mesh thread, so that the latch is past the horizontal mesh. Make sure the latch is in the open position, and the yarn is placed over the latch and under the hook (diagram 2).

diagram 2

4. Pull the hook back slightly toward you, and the latch will close over the yarn. Continue to pull the hook back under the horizontal mesh thread and through the yarn loop (diagram 3)

diagram 3

5. Pull the hook all the way through, then pull the yarn ends with your fingers to tighten the knot onto the mesh (diagram 4).

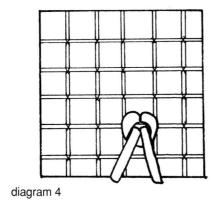

diagram 4

### To Hook the Rug

*Note:* If you are making our design, each square on the chart represents one knot to be made on one horizontal mesh thread; the different symbols represent the different colors and are explained by the key below the chart.

1. Hook colors row by row from bottom to top, working one piece of yarn in each horizontal mesh.

2. Continue to hook the rug row by row, always working from bottom to top. Change colors whenever indicated as you go across each row.

### To Finish the Rug

1. Remove the masking tape from the edges of the canvas and turn it wrong-side up on a table.

2. Trim the unstitched canvas edges to 2".

3. Fold the unstitched canvas to the back of your work and pin in place.

4. Using the heavy-duty thread and needle, stitch the hem to the wrong side of the rug.

5. Turn the rug right-side up and trim any long yarn ends so the surface is even.

### chart for hooked rug
one square = one knot

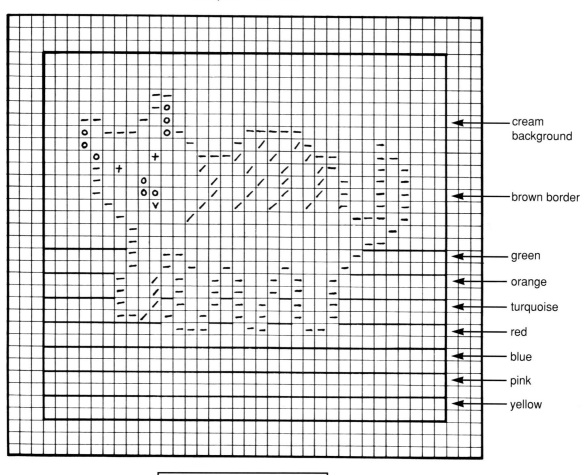

cream background

brown border

green

orange

turquoise

red

blue

pink

yellow

| o | pink | / | brown |
|---|------|---|-------|
| — | gray | | |
| v | red | + | blue |

12

*Stoneware Crock,*
circa 1860

# POTTERY

In early American households, jugs, jars, and crocks were used for storing food and beverages much the way we now use plastic containers. Local potters made these necessities, as well as all the plates, bowls, and mugs, and even flowerpots and roofing tiles, from the clay they dug and processed.

These simple, functional objects were formed on a potter's wheel, air-dried, then glazed and fired in a kiln (a special oven for pottery) at a high temperature for up to a day and a half. Glazes—mixtures of powdered metals, clay, sand, and water—added shine and color to the pots and helped to make the pottery watertight. The jug shown here is stoneware with a simple salt glaze. (The glaze forms when salt is thrown into the kiln as the jug bakes.) Stoneware, usually gray in color, was in demand because it was durable and nonporous.

Decorations, such as the distinctive cobalt-blue designs popular from 1825, gave the potters an outlet for their artistic impulses. Other methods of decoration were applying hand-formed clay leaves, fruit, and flowers, and cutting a design into wet clay with a sharp tool. Many individual potters have been identified by their characteristic styles and designs, and old pieces can be traced back to them.

# *Project:* CLAY POT

You don't need a potter's wheel or any complicated tools to make our clay pot. It's made from self-hardening clay, so there is no need to bake it in a professional kiln. However, this kind of clay cannot be used to hold liquids. Before beginning, read the directions on your package of clay so that you understand how to work with it and how long it will need to dry. Tiny, dollhouse-size pots can be formed around the end of your finger. Be sure to cover your work surface with newspapers so cleanup will be easy.

## Materials
- old table knife
- self-hardening clay
- plastic kitchen wrap
- rolling pin
- 3½"-4½" diameter container
- wooden modeling tool or Popsicle stick
- acrylic paints in colors of your choice
- assorted paintbrushes
- pencil
- paper
- masking tape
- acrylic varnish

## To Begin

Working on a newspaper-covered surface, use the knife to cut a wedge of clay from the block. Knead the clay by pressing it flat with the palms of your hands, folding it over and pressing again; repeat until it is very pliable. Shape it into a ball and cover it with plastic wrap to keep it soft.

## To Make the Pot

1. To make the base, take a piece of the kneaded clay and roll it out using the rolling pin (or pressing it flat with the heel of your hand) until it is about ⅜" thick.

2. Press the open end of the container into the clay to cut a circle. Peel away the excess clay (diagram 1).

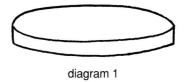

diagram 1

3. Using the palms of your hands, roll some of the clay into a coil or "snake" no more than ½" thick and long enough to fit around *and* on top of the edge of the base. Repeat to make several coils of the same size (diagram 2).

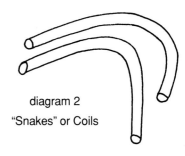

diagram 2
"Snakes" or Coils

4. Place one of the coils around the top of the base and join it into a ring; trim off any excess length with the knife (diagram 3).

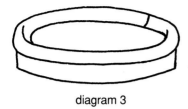

diagram 3

5. With the fingers of one hand inside the pot for support, use the modeling tool or the fingers of your other hand to smooth the outer edge into the base, also smoothing at the join (diagram 4).

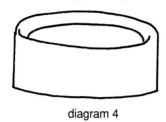

diagram 4

6. Next, smooth the inside of the coil onto the base.

7. Continue in this way to add coils, one at a time, directly on top of each other, until you have made the pot as high as you wish. Our pot measures about 3½" high. When smoothing the last coil, leave it slightly rounded to form the lip of the pot.

8. To make the handles, roll a thin coil, about ¼" thick. Cut two short pieces, curve them slightly, and attach them to each side of the pot, using little bits of clay for adhesive (diagram 5).

diagram 5

9. Let the pot dry completely.

**To Paint**

1. Using the acrylic paint, paint the inside and outside of the pot a solid color, and let the paint dry completely.

2. Using a pencil, trace or sketch a design of your choice on a piece of paper, making sure it will fit on your pot. Turn the paper over and lightly rub the pencil over the back of the design area.

3. Put the paper, design-side out, against the side of the pot and lightly tape it in place.

4. Draw over the design lines with the pencil; the pattern will transfer to the pot. Remove the paper and tape.

5. Paint the design in colors of your choice. Let the paint dry completely.

6. Give the pot a glossy finish by painting it with acrylic varnish; follow the manufacturer's directions.

**designs for clay pot**

*Doll: Mollie Bentley,* circa 1886

*Doll,* circa 1870

## RAG DOLLS

As far back as history goes children have played with dolls. In early America some dolls were very simple indeed—perhaps just a stick with a painted face, wrapped in a scrap of cloth.

Then, as now, the rag doll was a favorite. Rag dolls got their name because originally they were literally made from rags or scraps of leftover fabric. Worn clothing was recycled for many purposes. It provided pieces for patchwork quilts, strips for rugs, and—for lucky children—dolls. Rag dolls were made in all varieties: white and black, girls and boys, Indians, grandmothers, soldiers, and even frontiersmen.

As the country became more affluent, and people could afford to spend more money, these dolls were made from better materials and were dressed in fancy clothes. Sophisticated china heads made in Austria and Germany or wax heads from England could be attached to bodies made of fine cloth or leather and then dressed in the latest fashion.

# *Project:* RAG DOLL

You can make all three of these dolls from our basic patterns, or you can add your own special details and make the hair and clothes in different colors. Our dolls are Carlotta, who is dressed in lace and pearls; Lois, who protects herself from the sun with a straw hat; and Charlie, whose worn-out shirt sports a few patches.

You can sew these dolls by hand or with a sewing machine. If you want to sew by hand and do not know how, see the guide to stitches and the diagrams.

### Materials
- photocopies of patterns, or tracing paper
- pencil
- scissors for paper and fabric
- ¼ yd. fabric for each doll body: muslin or other similar-weight material
- straight pins
- acrylic paints and small paintbrush to paint faces
- ruler
- sewing machine or needle
- thread
- iron and ironing board
- fiberfill stuffing for body
- small amounts of black, red, and yellow yarn for hair
- small piece of cardboard
- ¼ yd. fabric for each dress (print or solid)
- assorted trimmings such as lace, beads, bow, and straw hat
- small snap for each doll
- scrap of fabric for trousers
- 6" length of ¼" elastic and 2 small safety pins for trousers
- pinking shears (optional)
- scrap of fabric for apron
- ribbon for apron

### To Begin
1. Make photocopies of the patterns, or use a pencil to trace them from the book onto tracing paper, including all markings.
2. Cut out the paper patterns.

### To Cut the Doll
1. Lay the muslin fabric right-side up on the table. Fold the two short edges toward the middle.
2. Place the body pattern piece on the fabric with the straight edge on one of the folds, and pin in place.
3. Pin the arm and leg pattern pieces to the same half of the fabric.
4. Cut out these pieces, then unpin the patterns.
5. Repeat on the other half of the fabric. You should have two body pieces and four arm and four leg pieces. Unfold the two body pieces, but leave the arms and legs in pairs as you cut them.

### To Paint the Face
1. Using a pencil, mark the facial features onto one side of the head, following our diagram.
2. Using the paints and small paintbrush, paint the features.
3. Let the paint dry.

### To Sew the Doll
*Note:* Always pin the pieces of fabric together with the right sides facing one another (inside out) unless the directions say to do otherwise. We have included ¼" seam allowances on all the patterns (that means you should stitch the pieces together ¼" from the cut edge). You can mark the seam line with a pencil if you want to.

1. Pin and then sew the two body pieces together around all the edges except the bottom. Use a backstitch if you are sewing by hand (see the guide to stitches).
2. As shown on the pattern, clip small Vs from the seam allowance; be careful not to clip the stitches. Clip into the curve at the neck as well. This will help the seam to lie smoothly when the doll is turned right-side out.
3. Turn the body right-side out and press the seam with the iron.
4. Fill the body with the loose stuffing; use the eraser end of the pencil to push the stuffing into the head, and fill firmly.

5. Turn under the bottom edges of the body ¼" and pin closed. Sew across, using an overcast stitch.

6. Pin the arm and leg pieces together in pairs. Leaving the top edges open, sew around the seam line, ¼" from the edges.

7. Clip the curves of the arms and legs in the same way you did the body, then turn them right-side out and press.

8. Stuff the arms and legs with loose stuffing. Turn open the edges of the arms under ¼" and pin closed. Sew across, using an overcast stitch.

9. Pin each arm to the body at the shoulder and sew in place, using an overcast stitch.

10. Turn open the edges of the legs under ¼" and pin closed, matching the seam lines at the center. Stitch closed as described above. Pin each leg to the lower edge of the body with the toes facing forward, and sew in place.

### To Make the Hair

*For black and red hair*

1. Wrap a single strand of yarn around a ruler, placing the strands close together; wrap the black hair for 6" and the red hair for 4".

2. With the yarn still on the ruler and using a needle and thread, backstitch the strands together along one edge of the ruler.

actual-size patterns for rag doll

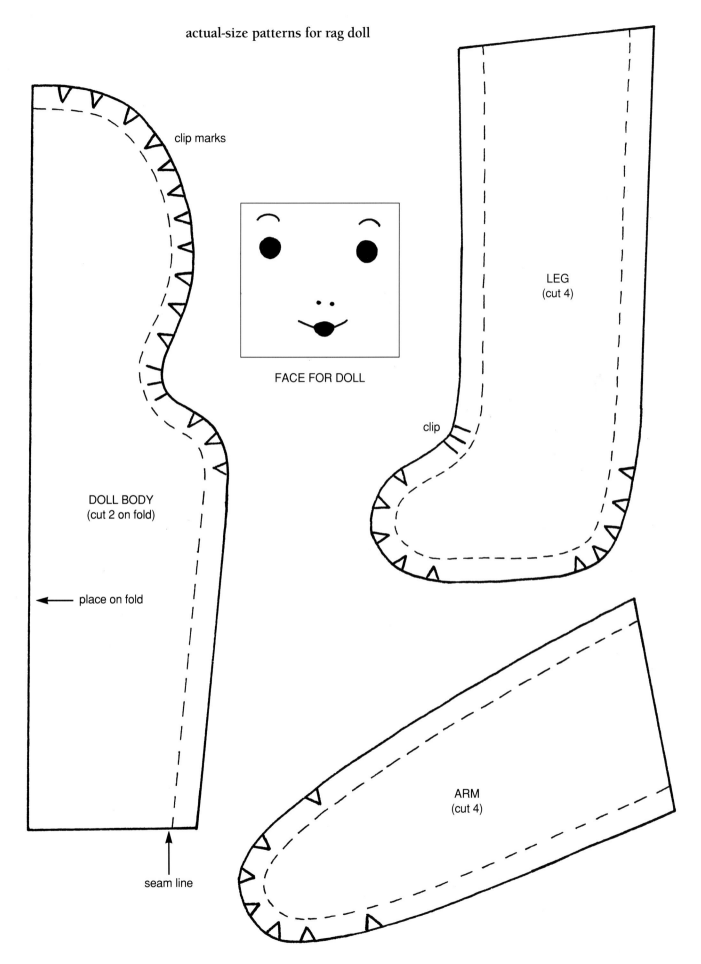

clip marks

FACE FOR DOLL

LEG
(cut 4)

clip

DOLL BODY
(cut 2 on fold)

place on fold

seam line

ARM
(cut 4)

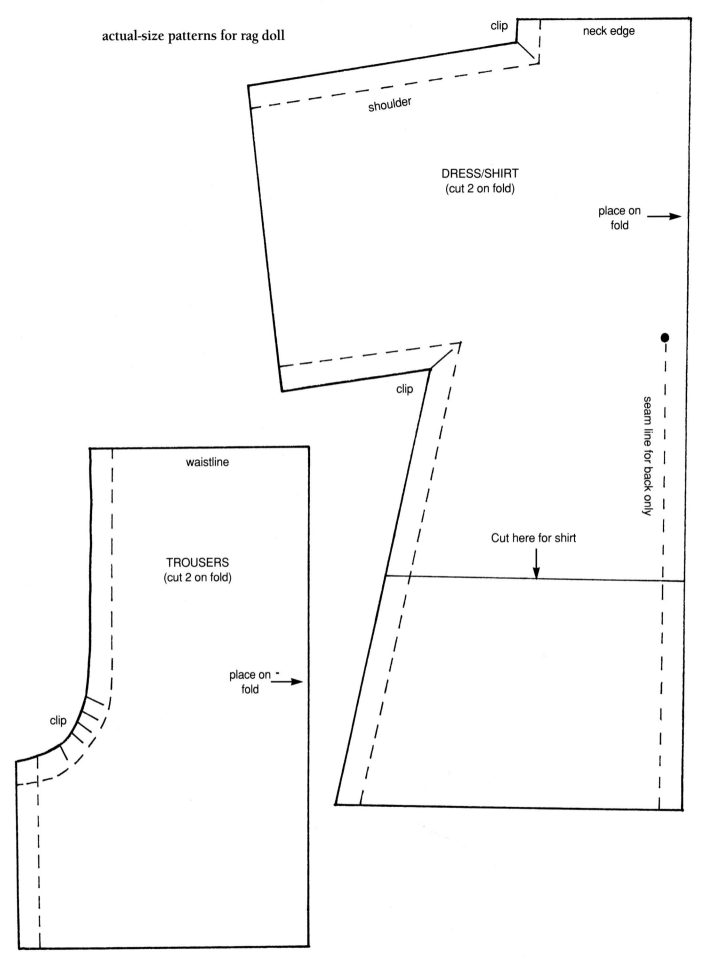

actual-size patterns for rag doll

clip

neck edge

shoulder

DRESS/SHIRT
(cut 2 on fold)

place on
fold

clip

seam line for back only

waistline

Cut here for shirt

TROUSERS
(cut 2 on fold)

place on
fold

clip

20

3. Slip the yarn off the ruler and pin the stitched edge to the seam along the top of the head. With matching thread sew it in place, using an overcast stitch.

*For yellow hair*

1. Cut a 7"-long piece of cardboard and loosely wrap twelve to eighteen loops of yarn over it. Carefully slip the yarn off the cardboard.

2. Wrap a short piece of yarn around the loops about 1½" from each end.

3. Twist the middle section of the yarn a few times and pin it to the seam along the top of the head. With matching thread, sew it in place with a few overcast stitches.

### To Make the Dress

1. Fold the dress fabric in half. Place straight side of the dress pattern along the fold. Pin in place and cut it out. This is the dress front.

2. Pin the pattern to the fabric again so that you can cut around all the edges. Cut it out, making two pieces. These are the dress back. Unpin the pattern.

3. Pin the dress back pieces together along the straight center back edge. Sew them together from the dot marked on the pattern to the bottom edge. Press this seam open and press the seam allowance on the edges above the dot to the wrong side as well.

4. Starting at the neck edge and stitching ⅛" from the fold, sew along the back opening to the center back seam, then turn and sew along the other side to the neck edge again.

5. Unfold the front of the dress and place it right-side up on the table. Place the back wrong-side up over it and pin the pieces together along the shoulders. Sew the shoulder seams and press them open.

6. Press the seam allowance at the sleeve hems to the wrong side. Sew the sleeve hems, stitching ⅛" from the fold. Add lace or other trim at this time.

7. Fold the dress along the shoulders so that it is inside out again, and pin the front to the back along each underarm/side seam. Sew these seams. Clip into the corner at each underarm, then press the seams open.

8. Press the seam allowance at the bottom of the dress to the wrong side. Sew around the bottom of the dress, stitching ⅛" from the fold. Add lace or other trim.

9. Press the seam allowance at the neck to the wrong side. Sew around the neck, stitching ⅛" from the fold. Add lace or other trim.

10. Try the dress on the doll, overlapping the back opening ¼" and pinning it closed.

11. Fit the front of the dress by pinning one small pleat at center front. Take the dress off the doll and sew the pleat, using one cross-stitch.

12. To finish, sew a small snap to the top of the back neck opening. Add sash, bow, lace, or other trim as you wish.

### To Make the Shirt

If you are making the shirt, cut the pattern on the marked line and follow the directions for the dress, above. Add patches and the button as you wish.

### To Make the Trousers

1. Lay the fabric on the table right-side up. Fold it so that you will be able to cut two pieces from the pattern, both with the long straight side on a fold. Pin and cut two pieces from the pattern.

2. Unpin the pattern but leave the pieces folded. Pin and sew each along the short straight edge below the curved edge. Press the seams open. These are the legs.

3. Turn one leg right-side out and slip it inside the other one, matching the seams. Pin and sew the legs together along the curved edge. Snip into the seam allowances along the curve, as shown on the pattern. Turn the trousers right-side out and press the seam open.

4. To form a casing for the elastic, press ½" around the waist to the wrong side. Sew around the waist ⅜" from the fold, leaving a 1" opening.

5. Pin a small safety pin to one end of the elastic. Insert the pin into the casing and use it to guide the elastic around the waist. Pin the free end of the elastic to the trousers with another pin so that you don't pull it in by mistake. When the safety-pinned end of the elastic pokes out of the casing, pin the two ends together, overlapping ¼", and sew them securely. Sew the 1" opening in the casing closed.

6. Finish the bottoms of the legs by trimming them with the pinking shears, or let them fray.

### To Make the Apron

1. Cut a piece of fabric 4" x 6" for the apron skirt and another piece 2" x 4" for the band. Cut two 12" lengths of ribbon for the ties.

2. Press a ¼" seam allowance on both 4"-long edges of the apron skirt to the wrong side and sew ⅛" from the fold. Repeat along one 6"-long edge.

3. Gather the other edge by making two rows of running stitches about ¼" from the edge and pulling the threads until the edge measures 3".

4. Press ¼" on one 4"-long edge of the band to the wrong side. Press ½" on each end of the band to the wrong side.

5. Pin and sew the gathered edge of the skirt to the other 4"-long edge of the band (with long raw edges even).

6. Press the band toward the seam, then fold it over the seam so that the folded edge meets the stitching. Tuck one end of each piece of ribbon into each end of the band and pin. Sew across one end of the band, along the seam over the gathers, and across the other end of the band, using small stitches.

### Guide to Stitches

*Backstitch:*

This stitch is used instead of a sewing machine to join two pieces of fabric. To start, insert the needle into the fabric and bring it up a very small distance away along the seam line at 1. For the first stitch only, insert the needle forward along the seam line at 2 and up at 3. The next stitch, 4, is taken backward along the seam line and in at the end of the previous stitch. Continue by bringing the needle up ahead a small distance and then closing the stitch backward.

*Overcast stitch:*

Use this stitch to close the doll body, arm, and leg openings and also to join the legs and arms to the body. Work the stitches from right to left, taking small diagonal stitches through both layers of material.

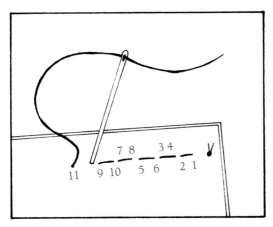

Backstitch

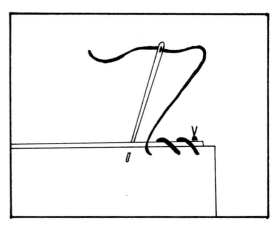

Overcast stitch

*Weather Vane: Squirrel*, circa 1797

*Weather Vane: Indian*, early nineteenth century

*Weather Vane: Horse*, late eighteenth century

*Weather Vane: Rooster,* late eighteenth century

## WEATHER VANES

Which way does the wind blow? In earlier times before the days of sophisticated weather-tracking satellites and meteorologists monitoring our climate, the farmer and the sailor relied on the weather vane to help them predict coming weather conditions.

The rooster, the most famous of weather vane characters, was used as early as the ninth century in Europe, on the roofs of churches, to ward off evil and proclaim good faith. Early American colonists, bringing this tradition with them, placed roosters atop barns and houses; however, they also used other designs.

Local craftsmen, farmers, and carpenters experimented with a variety of designs. In country areas inland, weather vanes took the form of cows, pigs, and horses, while on the coast fish, whales, and sailboats were common. Indians were also popular and the eagle became a patriotic theme around the mid-nineteenth century.

At first weather vanes were made from simple wooden planks; later they were cut from sheet iron, and still later they were fashioned of copper, and the designs were highly detailed.

# *Project:* WEATHER VANE MOBILE

Here are five traditional weather vane shapes for you to cut out, paint, and string together to make a mobile. We've antiqued ours by dabbing black paint over a solid color with a piece of dry sponge.

When the shapes are strung and hung from a rod, they will move gently in the air circulating in your room. They would also look good hanging individually as ornaments.

### Materials
- photocopies of patterns, or tracing paper
- pencil
- scissors
- poster board or oaktag
- craft knife
- cutting mat or protected work surface
- acrylic paints in assorted colors and black
- medium-wide paintbrush
- plastic plate for palette
- dry sponge
- paper towels
- clear acrylic spray finish (optional)
- sharp tool, such as a compass point or needle
- heavy-duty carpet thread or thin string
- large-eye needle
- one thin garden stake or dowel cut to 14" long
- quick-drying craft glue

### To Cut the Shapes
1. Make photocopies of the patterns, or use a pencil to trace them from the book onto tracing paper.
2. Cut out the paper patterns.
3. Place the patterns on the poster board and draw around them, using a pencil.
4. Cut out each shape using scissors. (You might find it easier to cut the more complicated shapes with the craft knife. To do this, put the poster board on the cutting mat or protected work surface, and carefully cut out the shapes with the knife.)

### To Paint the Shapes
1. Choose a color for one of the shapes and paint one side. Let the paint dry. Turn the shape over and paint the other side.
2. Repeat, painting each remaining shape a different color. Clean the paintbrush after each color. Let the paint dry completely.
3. Put a small amount of black paint in the plastic plate.
4. Cut a 1½"-square piece from the sponge. Dip one broad side into the paint, then tap it on paper towels to remove excess paint. To work best, the sponge should have very little paint on it and leave a mottled pattern on the paper.
5. Tap the sponge lightly over one side of one of the painted shapes.
6. Repeat to sponge-paint one side of each of the other shapes, adding more paint to the sponge as necessary. If the sponge becomes saturated, switch to a dry piece. Let the black paint dry.
7. Turn the shapes over and sponge-paint the other side. Let the paint dry completely.
8. Spray one side of the shapes with a light coat of clear acrylic spray. Let the spray dry, then repeat on other side (optional).

### To String the Mobile
*Note:* Refer to the photograph of the mobile.
1. Place each pattern shape on top of the corresponding painted shape. Using a compass point or needle, pierce a small hole through the shape at each X on the pattern.
2. Cut five 18" lengths of heavy-duty carpet thread.
3. Tie a knot at the end of one length and insert the other end through the hole at the top of the whale. Pull the string through and insert it into the hole at the bottom of the horse, measuring 6" of thread between the two shapes. Tie another knot and trim off the excess thread.
4. Knot one end of a second piece of thread and insert it into the hole at the top of the horse shape. Measure 12" of thread and tie it to the stake, 2" from one end.
5. Put a drop of craft glue on the knot to secure it to the stake and let dry.
6. String the squirrel and Indian in the same way, measuring 7" between the shapes and 9" between the stake and the Indian.

7. Tie them to the stake 2" from the end of the opposite side. Put a drop of glue on the knot on the stake and on each additional knot you make.

8. String the rooster by inserting a length of thread from one hole to the other, then tying it to itself. Knot the thread to the center of the stake, measuring 7" of thread.

9. Cut a 2' length of carpet thread and knot each end to an end of the stake.

10. Hang the mobile where it can swing freely.

**actual-size patterns for weather vane mobile**

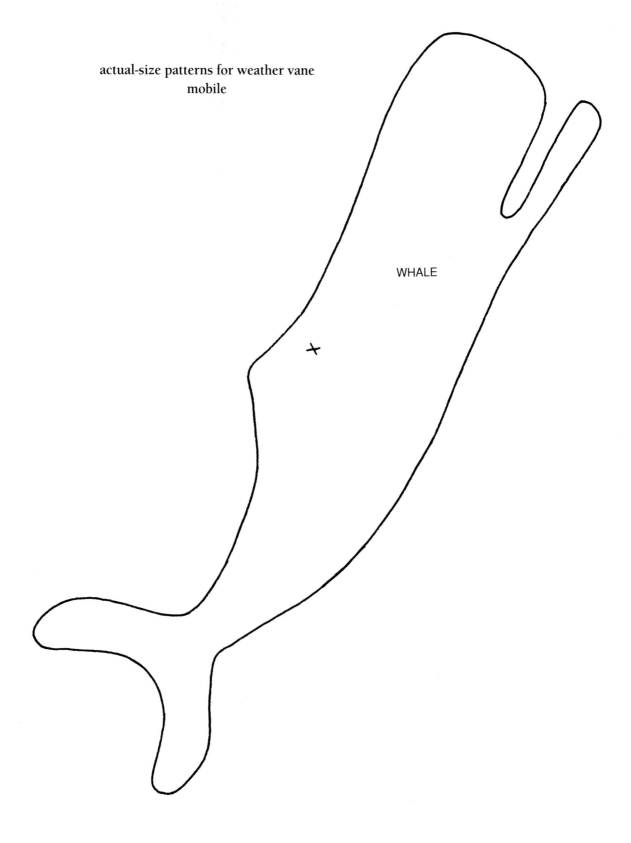

WHALE

INDIAN

ROOSTER

27

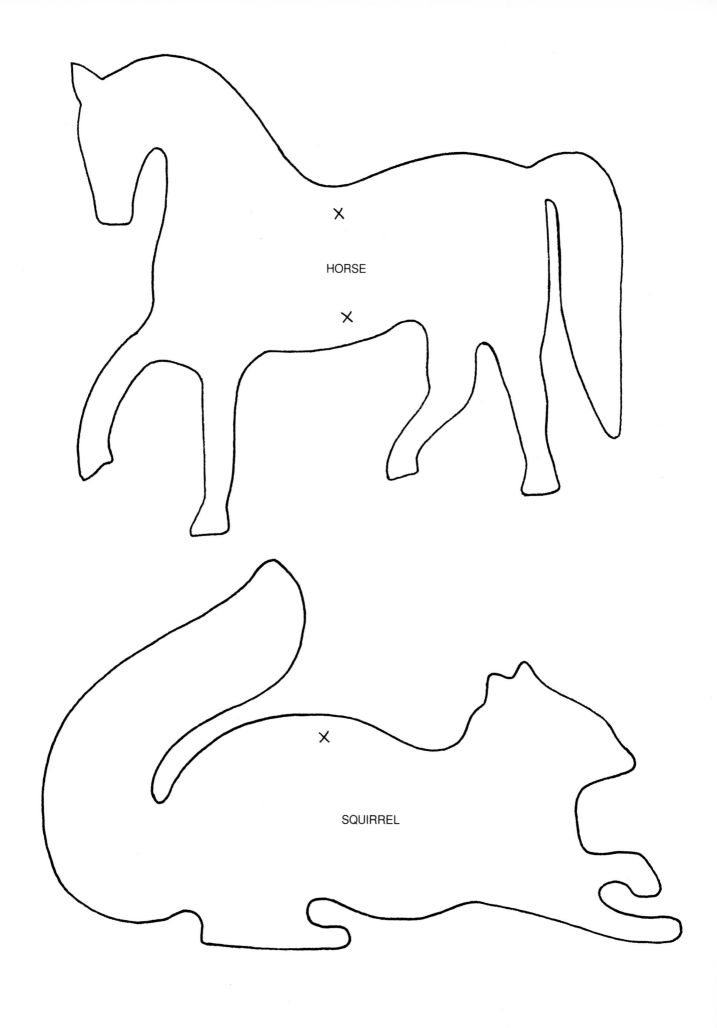

HORSE

SQUIRREL

*Sampler*, 1822

*Sampler*, 1813

# SAMPLERS

It is not unusual to see a sampler more than one hundred years old that was made by a child under twelve years of age! Because in colonial times there were no stores where ready-made clothing could be bought, stitchery was an important skill for children to learn. All clothes—shirts, pants, dresses, undergarments, and aprons—as well as quilts and coverlets were made at home or by a local seamstress or tailor.

A sampler served two purposes: it displayed both the needlework skill and the spelling ability of the maker. An eight-year-old girl would usually be skillful enough to create a master sampler for her parents to show off. Boys might also learn stitching too for careers in leather work or shoemaking.

One of the easiest stitches, a cross-stitch, is a simple X. Many samplers are made entirely from cross-stitches in threads of various colors. The alphabet, houses, trees, flowers, and even short sayings or mottoes, were all stitched into samplers.

## *Project:* CROSS-STITCH SAMPLER

Cross-stitching is simply making Xs with em-broidery thread on special cloth. It is really very easy, and the diagrams give a clear picture of how it is done.

The special cloth, usually called "Aida," is available at crafts and needlework stores. It is sold by "count," or the number of stitches you can make on it in a linear inch. For this project we used 6-count cloth, with large and easy-to-see stitches.

Ironing fusible interfacing to the back of the cross-stitch cloth makes it firm enough to stitch on without using a hoop and prevents the edges

from unraveling. You start and stop your stitching with knots.

### Materials

- iron and ironing board
- heavy-weight fusible interfacing in same size as cross-stitch cloth
- 6-count Aida or other cross-stitch cloth: 16" x 18" for large design, 5" square for small design
- ruler
- pencil
- small scissors

- embroidery floss: in colors shown in key for each chart
- large-eye tapestry or embroidery needle
- picture frame as desired

### To Prepare the Cloth

1. Using an iron and ironing board, fuse the interfacing to the cross-stitch cloth, following the manufacturer's directions. Make sure the fusible side is face down on the cross-stitch cloth.

*Note:* Most fusible fabrics require using steam. Do not move the iron back and forth. Instead, hold it in place for at least 10 seconds to form the bond, fusing a portion at a time until you have fused the whole cloth. A press cloth placed over the item to be fused is handy and prevents the mistake of fusing the bonding material to your iron!

### To Mark the Design

*Note:* Cross-stitch is worked from a charted design. Each symbol on the chart represents one stitch, and the different symbols represent the different colors. The key next to the chart shows which color to use for each symbol. Experienced cross-stitchers often work by counting the squares as they embroider, but beginners can mark the design onto the cloth with a pencil.

1. *For the large design,* hold the fabric vertically. At the upper-left corner, measure in 4½" down from the top and 4½" in from the side edge, and make a small mark with the pencil on the square of the cloth grid at this point. This will be the top-left stitch of the "a" in the alphabet.
*For the small design,* at one corner measure in 1" down from the top and 1" in from the side edge, and make a small mark with the pencil on the square of the cloth grid at this point. This will be the top left stitch of the "a."

2. Use a pencil to lightly mark the design onto the cross-stitch cloth. Each square on the chart corresponds to one square of the cloth grid, so count carefully and mark the cloth squares with Xs that correspond to the design on the chart. You'll see that you have a pencil version of your sampler design when you are finished, and all you will have to do is embroider a cross-stitch over each mark.

### CHART FOR SMALL SAMPLER
one square = one cross-stitch

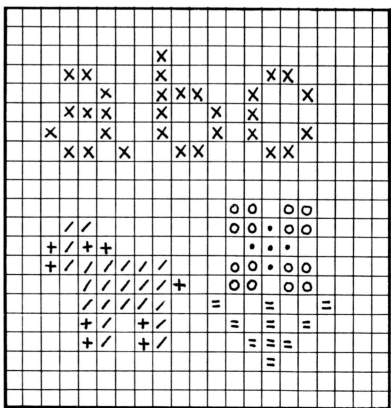

| + | black | = | green |
|---|---|---|---|
| / | white | • | pink |
| x | purple | o | turquoise |

31

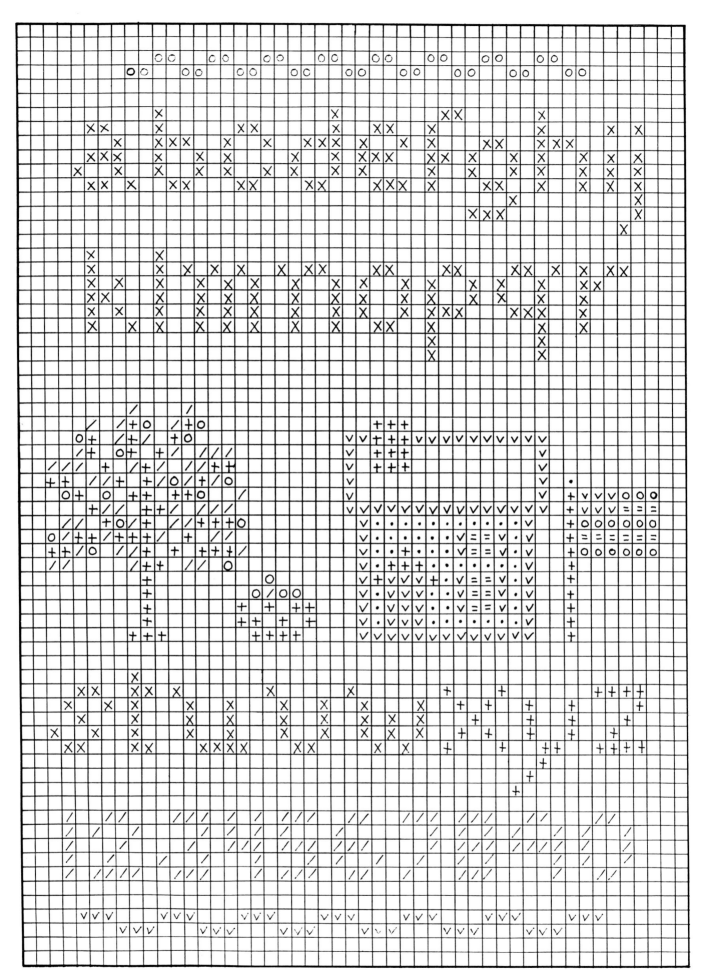

**CHART FOR LARGE SAMPLER**

*Note:* Pencil marks were often used on old samplers, the marks being covered by the embroidery threads. Any pencil-mark mistakes can be erased with a clean pink or white eraser.

### Preparing to Cross-Stitch

*Note:* Refer to diagrams 1 and 2 as you learn how to cross-stitch.

1. Cut a 14" length of embroidery floss. You will see that it is made of six strands of thread. We will use all six strands for stitching the six-count material.

2. Thread the tapestry needle and make a knot at one end of the floss.

*Note:* There are two easy ways to thread the needle. One is to snip the ends on a diagonal before inserting them into the eye; the other way is to wrap the end of the floss tightly over the end of the needle, slip it off, and insert the fold through the eye.

### To Cross-Stitch

1. Bring the needle up through the back of the cloth at the lower-left hole of one of the marked Xs (A on diagram 1). Insert the needle down through the hole at the upper right (B), pulling the floss all the way through. You have made one diagonal stitch, or half of a cross-stitch.

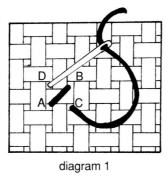

diagram 1

2. Bring the needle up through the lower-right hole (C), and down through the upper-left hole (D). You have completed one cross-stitch.

3. When you are making several stitches in a row, you can work all the diagonal halves first, and then go back and "cross" them. Diagram 2 shows this.

diagram 2

4. When the floss becomes too short to continue or you have worked all the stitches in that color, knot it on the back of the cloth and cut off the excess floss.

5. When you are stitching motifs that are not simple straight lines, take a minute to think about the best way to complete them so that you won't have lots of floating lengths of floss on the back of your sampler.

### To Cross-Stitch the Samplers

1. Even though you have marked the design on the cloth, you will need to refer to the chart and symbol key to see which colors to use for the different motifs.

2. It does not really matter where you begin to stitch. Some people like to begin in the middle, some at one corner. The important thing is to make a plan so that you can work logically; for instance, stitching one row of the alphabet from left to right.

*Note:* If your embroidery floss begins to twist up or knot, drop the needle and let it hang. You will see it spin around and untwist itself.

| | |
|---|---|
| x black | v blue |
| + brown | = white |
| o red | • yellow |
| / green | |

Key for Large Sampler

*Cradle, 1780*

*Stenciled Chair, 1829*

# STENCILED FURNITURE

Stenciling could be called a shortcut to painting. The stencil is a cutout design in a heavy paper that is placed over the surface to be decorated; paint is applied with a stiff brush, and when the stencil is lifted there is a perfect image.

The stencil technique has been known since ancient times. Early Americans used it in decorating chairs, dressers, stools, trunks, trays, and clocks, as well as walls, floors, and coverlets.

Typical motifs were fruit, leaves, birds, and the horn of plenty, or cornucopia. In many cases, stenciled motifs were painted on the popular "Hitchcock Chair," named after the manufacturer in Connecticut. This simple, sturdy chair has a wide slat across the back, a perfect space for a stenciled motif.

Usually, these chairs were first painted solid black and then the decoration was applied in gold, copper, and silver paint. Linear motifs, also in these colors, outlined the seat, legs, and back of the chairs.

# Project: STENCILED STOOL

Although you can buy ready-cut stencils at an arts or crafts supply store, making your own is not difficult. There are several types of stencil papers to choose from. White wax stencil paper is very easy to use, but clear acetate is also popular because it is transparent. Brown oiled-manilla stencil paper is very sturdy but can be a bit difficult to cut. Stencils can be used over and over again.

You can trace the patterns from this book, or you might like to look around your yard and home to find other interesting leaves and objects to use as designs for your project.

## Materials
- acetate or stencil paper
- scissors
- pencil
- photocopies of designs, or tracing paper
- masking tape
- thick pile of newspapers or cutting mat to protect work surface
- craft knife
- wooden stool (or other object to decorate), painted a solid color if desired
- white drawing paper
- small jars or squeeze bottles of acrylic craft paint in colors of your choice
- plastic plates for palette
- stencil brush for each color (or rinse and dry brush after using each color)
- paper towels
- fine paintbrush
- acrylic varnish

## To Transfer Stencil Designs
*Acetate*

1. For each pattern that you want to make into a stencil, cut a piece of acetate about 2"–3" bigger in each direction than the pattern shape.

2. Using a pencil, trace each pattern from the book right onto the acetate. Be sure that each shape is centered in the acetate.

*White wax stencil paper*

1. For each pattern that you want to make into a stencil, cut a piece of stencil paper about 2"–3"

bigger in each direction than the pattern shape.

2. Make photocopies of the patterns or use a pencil to trace them from the book onto tracing paper.

3. Tape the patterns to a windowpane. Tape a piece of the stencil paper over one of the patterns; be sure it is centered in the stencil paper.

4. Using a pencil, trace the shape onto the stencil paper. In the same way, trace the rest of the shapes onto stencil paper.

*Brown oiled-manilla*

1. For each pattern shape, cut the stencil paper as described above.

2. Trace the patterns from the book or make photocopies as above.

3. To transfer your design to oiled-manilla, place a piece of light-colored transfer paper between the oiled-manilla and the traced design. With a pencil, draw over each design, pressing firmly.

## To Cut Stencils

Place a marked piece of the stencil paper on a cutting mat or a surface protected with newspapers. Using the craft knife, carefully cut out the design. Repair any overcut lines by taping them closed with a little masking tape. Repeat to cut out all the designs.

## Planning Your Design

1. Create your design by outlining the shapes with a pencil onto a piece of tracing paper the same size as the stool.

2. Transfer the design to the stool by placing the tracing-paper design on the stool and slipping the stencils in place under the design.

3. Mark a few points of each stencil lightly onto the stool with a pencil.

4. Repeat for each stencil in the design.

5. When you have marked all the stencils, remove the tracing paper.

## To Paint the Stencils

If you have never painted a stencil before, experiment on plain white drawing paper before painting the stool.

*Note:* To prevent painting the wrong color into closely adjoining parts of a design, you can temporarily block them off with a bit of masking tape. Paint the untaped part as explained below, then uncover the taped part and continue.

1. Put a small amount of the first color of paint on a plastic plate. Holding a dry brush straight up and down, dip the ends into the paint. Tap the brush on newspaper or paper towels to remove excess paint. To work best, the brush should have very little paint on it.

2. Line up the first stencil with the pencil marks you made on the stool. Hold the stencil in place with one hand, or lightly tape down the edges in one or two places.

3. Paint the stencil using an up-and-down tapping motion, painting around the edges of the stencil first, then filling in the center.

4. As the paint dries, you can add additional layers until it is as light or as dense as you would like it.

5. Lift the stencil after you have finished painting it.

6. Continue adding designs one at a time, letting the paint dry after each design. (Don't overlap the stencil on wet paint. If your next design is close, let the paint dry before going on.)

7. When all the designs have been painted and are dry, you can add details like the ladybug's spots, freehand, using the small paintbrush.

### To Finish

When the designs and details are complete and the paint is thoroughly dry, you can paint a coat of acrylic varnish on the stool to protect your work, following the manufacturer's directions.

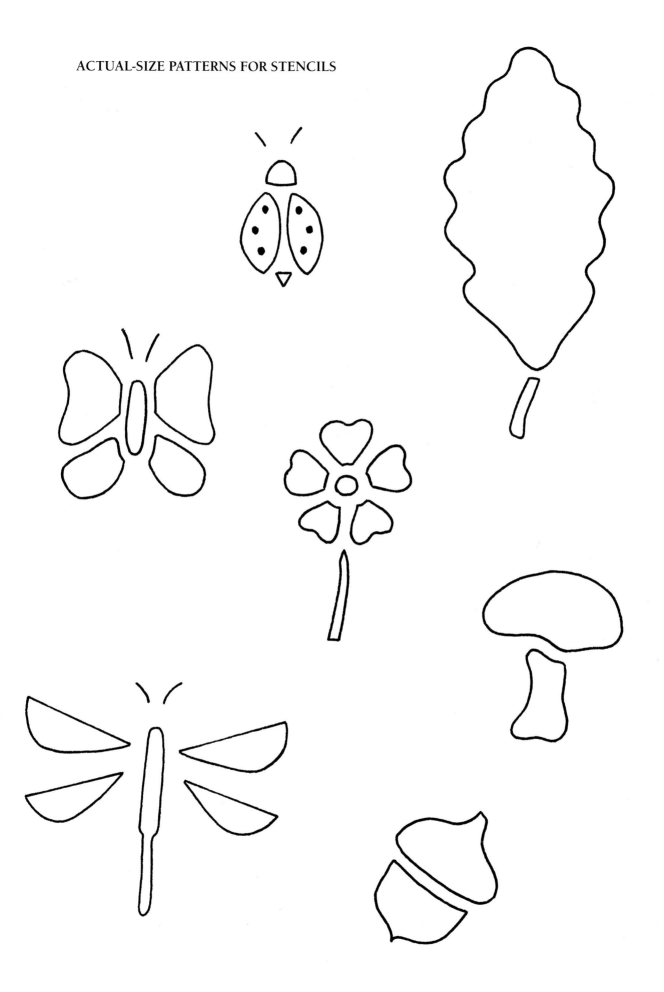

*Bandbox*, 1826

## BANDBOX

Imagine how long these pretty, paper-covered cardboard pieces of luggage would last today! Wildly popular by 1825, bandboxes fell out of use by the mid-nineteenth century as traveling Americans came to need sturdier suitcases for their adventures by coach, train, and boat.

A bandbox is basically a cardboard box covered in pretty paper and lined with newspaper. Originally such boxes stored men's shirt collars, called "bands," hence the name. To entice customers, printers who made the covering paper began designing all sorts of novelty scenes besides the allover florals. The scenic design called "Windmill Railroad," pictured above, is from circa 1830 and commemorates the advent of the railroad.

During the height of their popularity, these boxes were used by women to carry dainty accessories such as silk flowers, jewelry, scarves, ribbons, gloves, and hairpins. In New England, young women working in mill factories began buying these luxury boxes as status symbols, much as people today favor trendy, fashionable brands of luggage.

# *Project*: BANDBOX

Bandboxes are a lot of fun to make, and there are many attractive wrapping papers to choose from for covering your box. If you give one to a friend with another gift inside, there is no need to wrap it again. Just tie the bandbox with a pretty bow, and make a matching gift card from a bit of extra paper. If your wrapping paper has an allover pattern you can cut it in any direction, but take time to plan where a stripe or an unusual design will appear on the lid and sides of the box.

## Materials
- photocopies of patterns, or tracing paper
- pencil
- poster board (about 12" x 20" per box)
- scissors
- quick-drying craft glue, or white glue
- paper clips
- wrapping paper (one 19" x 27" sheet will cover 3 boxes)
- ruler
- glue stick

## To Cut and Assemble the Box

*Note:* The box bottom and lid are made the same way.

1. Make photocopies of the patterns, or use a pencil to trace them from the book onto tracing paper.

2. Cut out the paper patterns.

3. Place the patterns on the poster board and, holding them firmly in place, carefully draw around them, using a pencil.

4. Cut out the pieces.

5. Fold the flap extensions toward the inside of the box along the dotted lines, as shown on the pattern. Then fold the sides along the dotted lines toward the inside of the box.

6. Put craft glue on the outside of the flap extensions, then glue them to the inside of the box sides. Use paper clips to secure them while the glue is drying, and wipe off any excess glue.

7. Let the glue dry completely.

## To Cover the Box Bottom

1. Cut a strip of wrapping paper that measures

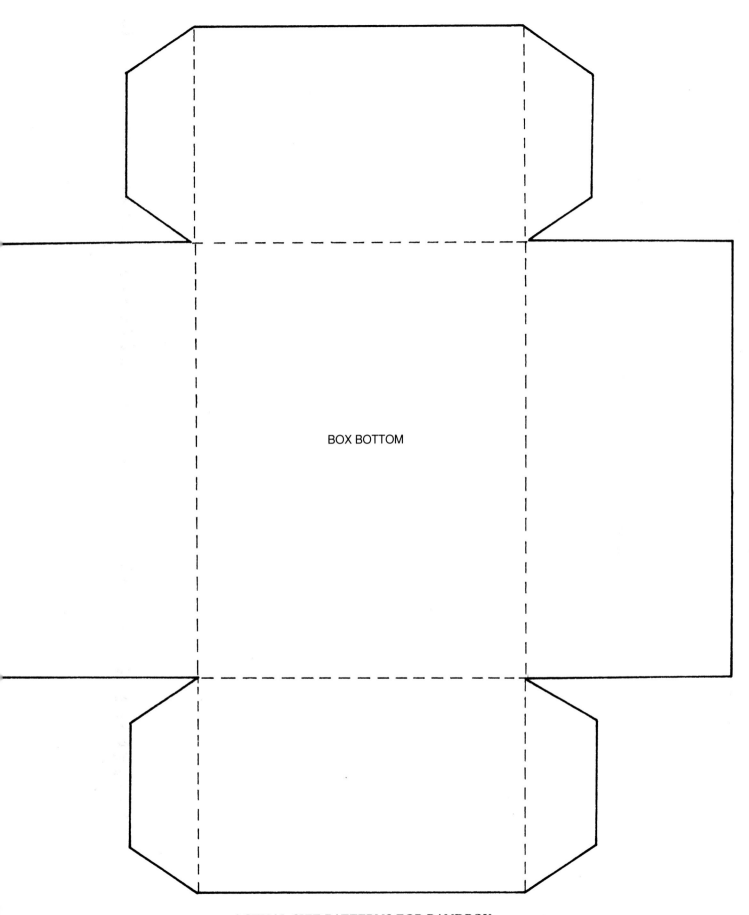

BOX BOTTOM

**ACTUAL-SIZE PATTERNS FOR BANDBOX**

Cut on solid lines
Fold on dotted lines

the box's height plus 1" (for the paper's width), by the perimeter (the distance around the box) plus ½" (for the length). If you are using our pattern, this strip should be 3¼" x 16¾".

2. Place the strip wrong-side up on the table. Using a pencil and ruler, draw a line parallel to and ½" from each long edge.

3. Using the glue stick, begin to spread glue on the outside of the box as follows: First spread glue over one half of one end of the box.

4. Position this glue-covered area over the end of the strip of paper so that the top and bottom edges of the box fit between the two marked lines. Smooth the paper with your fingers.

5. Spread glue on an adjacent side of the box and rotate it onto the strip. Press as before.

6. Continue to glue and rotate the box in this manner until all four sides are covered with paper, overlapping ½" at the end.

7. With the scissors, carefully clip the paper at each corner where it extends beyond the top and bottom of the box; clip right up to the box.

8. Place the box on its side on the table and spread glue on the paper where it extends over the top, then fold it over the edge and press it to the inside of the box. Repeat at the top of the other three sides.

9. In the same way, glue the paper extensions to the bottom of the box.

### To Cover The Box Lid

1. Cover the side of the lid in the same way you covered the bottom. The wrapping paper strip for the sides of the top should measure 1¾" x 17½".

2. For the top, place the lid on the wrong side of the wrapping paper. Trace around it using a pencil and cut out the shape.

3. Spread glue on the top of the lid. Place the paper over it and gently press it in place, matching the edges.

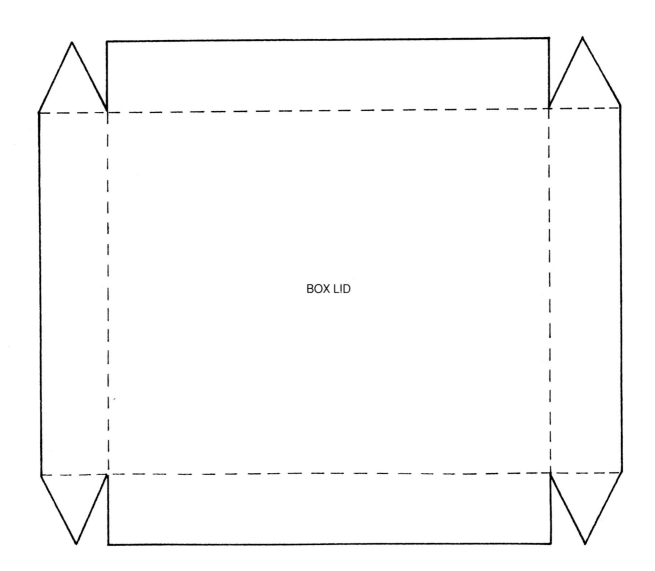

BOX LID

*Quilt Block*, 1870

# APPLIQUÉ QUILTS

In early American households everything the family needed had to be made from lengths of cloth either woven at home on a loom or, when possible, purchased. No snip of fabric was wasted; scraps were used for quilts, rag rugs, and lastly, for dolls and doll clothes.

Patchwork quilts were made from leftover bits of fabric stitched together in patterns, while appliqué quilts used carefully shaped bits of fabric sewed in designs onto a large piece of plain background fabric. Sometimes the patchwork and the appliqué method were combined in the same quilt.

Often the plain background fabric was divided into sections—nine, twelve, sixteen, or even twenty squares—which were then appliquéd with the same, similar, or different motifs. Each motif could be made of many separate little pieces of fabric, carefully stitched one by one.

When the appliqué quilt top was completed, it was decoratively stitched, or quilted, to a middle layer, the batting, and a plain bottom cloth. Frequently, groups of women and girls would get together for quilting parties called "bees," probably so named either because the participants were as busy as bees, or because they were buzzing like bees with gossip!

## *Project:* APPLIQUÉ PILLOW

Try these easy no-sew appliqués of strawberries and mice, and make them into pillows when you are finished. For this project, the appliqué shapes are cut from scraps of fabric and then fused to the white background with a special bonding material and an iron. Instead of traditional hand sewing with embroidery thread, you'll work with dimensional craft paints that come in "writer-tip" tubes to outline and embellish the appliqués. The paint is also used to make the stems of the strawberries as well as the mouse whiskers.

### Materials
•photocopies of patterns, or tracing paper
•pencil
•scissors
•6" x 6" scraps of fabric: reds, greens, and grays

•paper-backed fusible craft bond
•iron and ironing board
•white paper
•white cotton background fabric: two pieces 15" square for large pillow, two pieces 13" square for small pillow
•"writer-tip" acrylic craft paints: black, yellow, and green
•pins
•sewing machine or needle
•thread
•pillow forms: 14" square for large pillow, 12" square for small pillow

### To Make the Appliqué Pieces
1. Make photocopies of the patterns, or use a pencil to trace them from the book onto tracing paper. Patterns that are not symmetrical will be re-

versed when finished; turn these patterns over when marking out if desired.

2. Cut out the patterns.

3. Fuse each of the 6" x 6" pieces of fabric to a 6" x 6" piece of paper-backed craft bond with an iron, following the manufacturer's directions.

4. Decide which shapes you want from each fabric scrap by following our design, or draw several of each piece so that you have plenty to arrange when you make your own design.

5. Place the patterns on the paper side of the fused material, and draw around each shape using a pencil.

6. Cut out all of the appliqué shapes around the pencil lines.

### To Make the Appliqué Design

1. Sketch your design on a piece of white paper by drawing around the pattern pieces and adding details such as stems or whiskers. Follow our design or create your own. (Draw your design

within a 14" x 14" square for the large pillow and a 12" x 12" square for the small pillow, leaving ½" blank at each edge. Later, the ½" remaining on each edge of the white fabric will be needed for the seam allowance when you sew the pillow together.)

2. Transfer the design to the white fabric by placing one piece of white fabric right-side up over your sketch. Center it and use a pencil to lightly copy the design onto the material.

3. Peel the paper backing from the shapes and, one by one, put them in place and fuse to the white fabric with the iron, following the manufacturer's directions.

### To Paint the Details

*Note:* It is a good idea to practice painting on a scrap of fabric or a piece of paper so that you learn to control the paint.

1. When all the shapes have been fused in place you can begin to paint around the designs, adding

## ACTUAL-SIZE PATTERNS FOR APPLIQUÉS

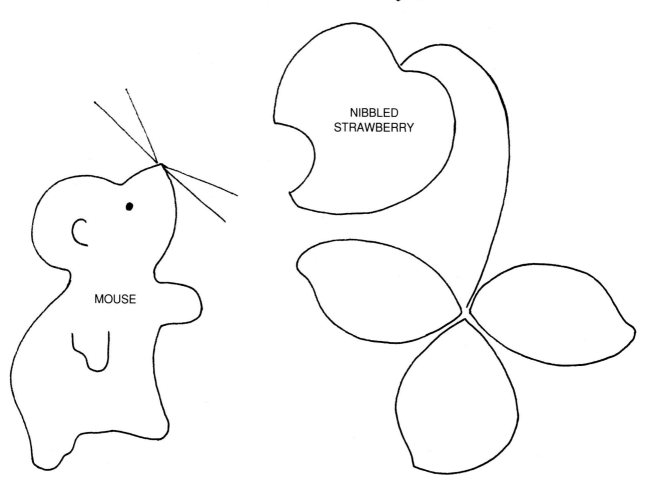

NIBBLED
STRAWBERRY

MOUSE

"stitches," stems, and whiskers, following the directions on the paint tubes.

2. Begin in the center of the design, working with one color at a time. Work carefully so that you don't accidentally smear the paint. Let the paint dry completely before applying the next color.

### To Make the Pillows

1. Place the appliquéd fabric right-side up on the table. Place the other piece of white fabric wrong-side up on top of it, matching the edges.

2. Pin along three sides, leaving the bottom edge unpinned.

3. Sew around the three pinned sides, ½" from the edge.

4. Trim the seam allowance to ¼" and turn the pillow right-side out.

5. Insert the pillow form in the pillow, turn under the bottom edge and pin it closed. Sew the pillow closed by hand, using very small overcast stitches.

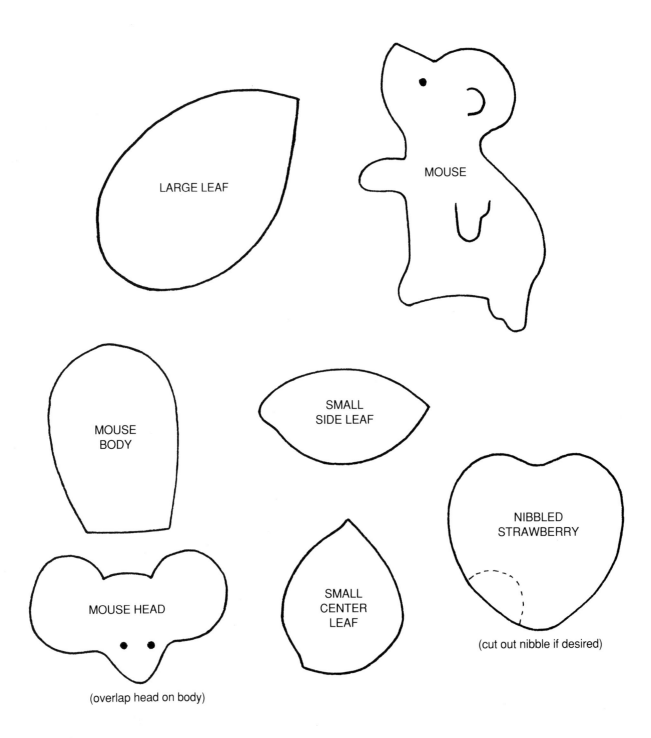

LARGE LEAF

MOUSE

MOUSE BODY

SMALL SIDE LEAF

NIBBLED STRAWBERRY

MOUSE HEAD

SMALL CENTER LEAF

(cut out nibble if desired)

(overlap head on body)

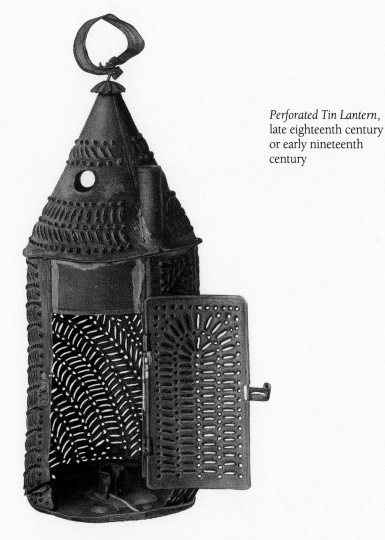

*Perforated Tin Lantern*, late eighteenth century or early nineteenth century

# LANTERN

Candlelight was the most common means of illumination in early American houses, and the making of candles and candle holders was an important part of colonial life. People went to bed soon after dark as candles were valuable and used sparingly.

Simple candle holders were made of wood or pottery; more elaborate ones were made of glass or metals like brass and silver.

New England craftsmen were known for candle holders with a protective case which were called lanterns. Perhaps most familiar to us is the "Paul Revere" lantern, which is made from a sheet of pierced tin formed into a cylinder with a conical top.

When candlelight shines softly through the decorative punched pattern of a Paul Revere lantern, it glows with a lacy effect.

## *Project:* PIERCED LANTERN

You can make an open-top lantern with a pierced design from an inexpensive foil baking pan. The pan can be easily cut with household scissors, left silver or painted, and punched with simple tools. When you are finished, slip your lantern over a 2" votive candle in a glass holder.

Children should work on this project with an adult who can point out which tools to use and how to handle them safely. The cut edges of the foil pan are sharp before they are covered with masking tape, and the punching must be done with care.

**Materials**
- 6" ruler
- pencil
- 9½"-square foil baking pan
- ½"-wide masking tape
- work gloves
- scissors
- newspapers
- spray paint (optional)
- photocopies of pattern, or tracing paper
- piece of corrugated box (to place under work when piercing)
- awl or compass point
- small screwdriver
- four paper fasteners

### *To Cut the Lantern Shape from the Pan*

*Note:* The outside of the pan will become the outside of the lantern.

1. Using the ruler and pencil, draw two parallel lines 6" apart across the central area of the inside of the pan. Continue the lines from the sides across the bottom and up the opposite sides, avoiding the pleated corners of the foil pan (diagram 1). You may want to mark the inside

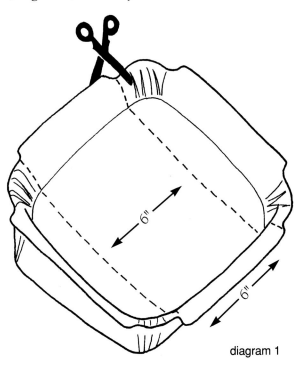

diagram 1

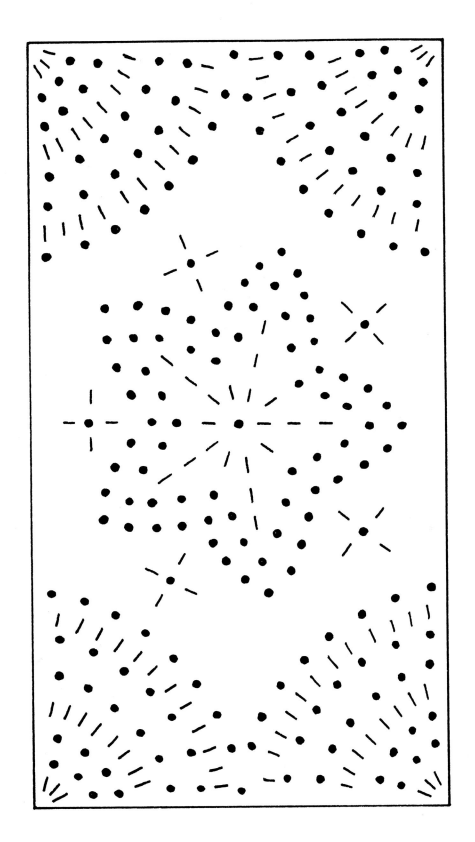

**ACTUAL-SIZE PATTERN FOR PIERCED LANTERN**

Pierce dash marks with small screwdriver
Pierce dots with awl or compass point

with a small piece of tape so you don't get confused later.

2. Wearing work gloves for protection from sharp edges, carefully cut along each line, cutting away two sides and all four corners. (Put aside these pieces for practicing your piercing technique later.)

3. Cover the long cut edges of the 6" wide panel with lengths of masking tape.

4. Using the ruler and a pencil, mark and score fold lines ¾" from each edge.

5. Fold the foil edges along these lines toward the inside.

### To Paint

1. Paint on a newspaper-covered surface in a well-ventilated place, or outdoors.

2. Place the foil panel tape-side down. Spray paint, following the directions on the can. Let the paint dry completely.

### To Transfer the Pattern

1. Make a photocopy of the pattern, or use a pencil to trace it from the book onto tracing paper.

2. Cut out the paper pattern on the rectangular outline.

3. Place the foil panel with the outside (painted side) down on the corrugated board on top of your protected work surface.

4. Center the pattern on the foil and secure the side edges with small pieces of masking tape.

5. Transfer the entire design by pressing through the pattern with a compass point or sharp pencil so that an impression is made on the foil underneath. Lift one edge of the pattern and make sure the design appears completely. Fill in any part you missed and remove the pattern.

6. Test the punching method on one of the narrow strips of foil you set aside. Place it on a corrugated board on your work surface, then experiment to see how much pressure you have to put on the small screwdriver and the awl or compass point to pierce the foil.

7. Place the foil panel on the corrugated board and, using the small screwdriver, carefully pierce through the foil on the dash marks. Then pierce the dots with the awl or compass point.

### To Form the Lantern

1. With the outside (painted side) facing you, form a cylinder by overlapping the ends. Tape them together temporarily.

2. Place the overlapped section on top of the corrugated work surface and punch two holes side by side and about ¾" from each end of the cylinder (diagram 2).

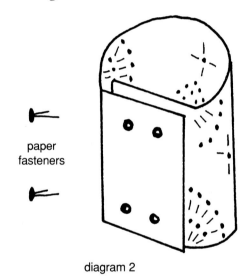

paper fasteners

diagram 2

3. Insert a paper fastener from outside to inside through one of the holes, open the prongs, and bend them flat against the inside. Repeat, putting a fastener in each remaining hole. Remove the tape.

*Doll: Harlequin Dancing Figure,* circa 1800

## JUMPING JACK

This dancing figure, dressed like a Harlequin (a comic character clad in multi-colored jacket and tights), is originally of French origin. At first dancing dolls were made to amuse children, but in France at the court of Louis XV (1710–1774), they were popular as entertainment for adults.

Called *Pantins* by the French after a small town outside Paris famous for its dancing, these toy figures were often painted to represent clowns, dancers, shepherds, shepherdesses, or even a simple pastry cook! During the reign of Louis XV, well-known artists painted them to resemble famous people, but *Pantins* were also made and painted by ordinary folk to represent ordinary folk. In America we call these toys "jumping jacks."

Made from sturdy board or wood, the jumping jack has limbs that are attached separately and can swivel. These toy figures can be made to dance by pulling the strings that are joined at the back and the arms and legs.

# *Project:* JUMPING JACKS

Here are two dancing dolls, or *Pantins*, for you to cut out and decorate—a Harlequin and a Ballerina. When you see how easy they are to string and make dance, you'll want to create a whole troupe and stage a show.

Perhaps you will want to design your own costumes, or make a dancing doll that looks like a friend or a famous person. Use your imagination—you can even make a dancing pumpkin for Halloween or an Uncle Sam for the Fourth of July.

## Materials
• photocopies of patterns, or tracing paper
• pencil
• scissors
• poster board
• single-hole punch
• sharp tool, such as a compass point or needle
• string or heavy-duty carpet thread
• large-eye needle
• four paper fasteners for each doll
• assorted trims, such as felt scraps, pom-poms, rickrack, ribbons, beads, or glitter
• felt-tipped markers
• craft glue
• large bead (about ½" diameter)

## To Cut the Doll
1. Make photocopies of the patterns, or use a pencil to trace them from the book onto tracing paper. Be sure to trace all the detail lines.
2. Cut out the paper patterns. Punch the large dots with the hole punch, and pierce the small ones with the compass point or needle so that you will be able to mark through them with a pencil. Set aside the patterns for the crown and cap.
3. Put the patterns on the poster board and draw around them, using a pencil. Make a mark through each of the holes.
*Note:* For each doll you will need to draw one body and one pair of arms and legs.
4. Cut out all of the pieces.
5. Punch the large marked dots with the hole punch, and pierce the small ones with the compass point or needle.

6. Before going any further, use the needle to thread a 2' length of string or thread through the small hole at the top of the doll's head. Pull the string halfway through and tie the ends together in a knot.

## To Decorate the Doll
Refer to the photo for ideas on how to decorate the doll. You can "paint" on the clothing with felt-tipped markers, or cut shapes from felt or fabric. Use the same patterns for the clothing that you used for the body, arms, and legs; and use the cap and crown patterns as well. We used a combination of markers and trims.
1. If you're using markers, sketch the desired patterns lightly with pencil first, then fill in with color.
2. If you're using felt, place the pattern piece on the felt, then draw around the pattern (marking off the head, hands, and feet as necessary) and cut it out. Glue the clothing onto the doll pieces, cutting out any holes that you may have covered.
3. Use markers to draw on the facial features.
4. Glue on any small trims that you wish to use. Be sure not to apply any trims to the tops of the arms or legs near the punched holes.

## To Assemble the Doll
1. Attach the arms and legs to the body by placing paper fasteners front to back through the body, then front to back through the corresponding limbs.
2. Open the prongs of the fasteners and bend them loosely against the back of each limb, allowing the limbs to swing free.
3. When the arms and legs are attached, place the doll face down on your worktable. Refer to the diagram as you string the doll.
4. Thread the needle and knot one end. Insert the needle through the small hole at the top of one arm, across the back of the doll, and through the small hole at the top of the other arm. Knot the thread to secure, and trim off excess.
5. Attach a second thread between the legs in the same way.

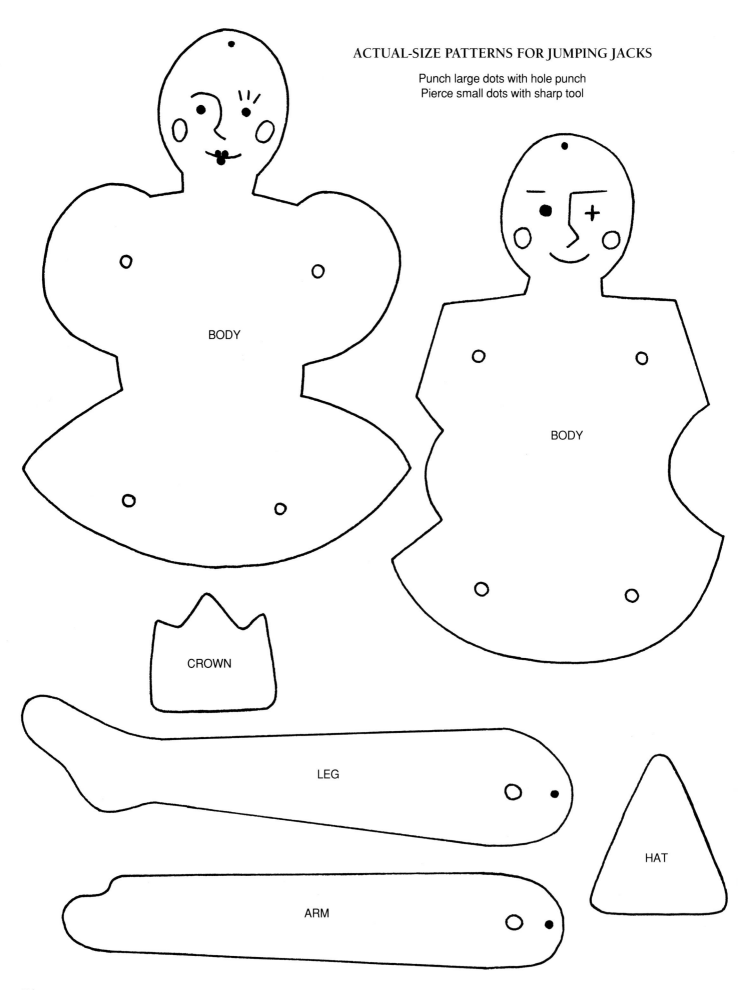

ACTUAL-SIZE PATTERNS FOR JUMPING JACKS
Punch large dots with hole punch
Pierce small dots with sharp tool

BODY

BODY

CROWN

LEG

ARM

HAT

54

**DIAGRAM FOR STRINGING**
(back view)

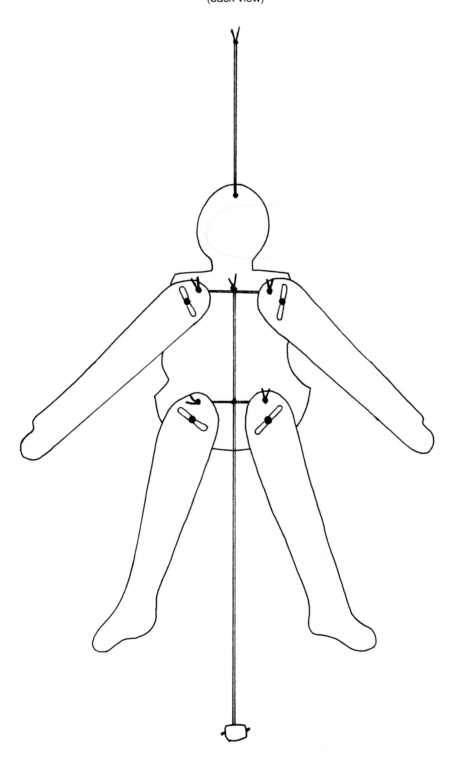

6. Cut a 2' length of thread. Fold it in half, and tie the ends to the center of the thread between the arms, and also to the center of the thread between the legs.

7. Thread a bead onto the bottom of the 2' length of string, and tie to secure. Hold the string above the doll's head, and with your other hand, pull gently on the bead to make it dance.

# LIST OF INDEX OF AMERICAN DESIGN ILLUSTRATIONS

*Bandbox,* 1826
Rendered by Jessie M. Youngs,
c. 1940
watercolor, gouache, and graphite
0.223 x 0.299 m (8¾ x 11¾ in)
National Gallery of Art, Washington
Index of American Design
1943.8.8414 (NYS-co-12)

*Cradle,* 1780
Rendered by Chris Makrenos,
c. 1940
watercolor, gouache, and pen and
ink
0.330 x 0.391 m (13 x 15⅜ in)
National Gallery of Art, Washington
Index of American Design
1943.8.11229 (MICH-fu-32)

*Doll,* c. 1870
Rendered by Mina Lowry, c. 1936
watercolor, graphite, and gouache
0.299 x 0.229 m (11¾ x 9 in)
National Gallery of Art, Washington
Index of American Design
1943.8.11221 (NYC-mscl-toys-60)

*Doll: Harlequin Dancing Figure,*
c. 1800
Rendered by Mina Lowry, c. 1936
watercolor, gouache, and graphite
0.289 x 0.229 m (11⅜ x 9 in)
National Gallery of Art, Washington
Index of American Design
1943.8.11230 (NYC-mscl-toys-46)

*Doll: Mollie Bentley,* c. 1886
Rendered by Josephine C. Romano
and Edith Towner, 1936
watercolor, graphite, and pen and
ink
0.357 x 0.267 m (14¹⁄₁₆ x 10½ in)
National Gallery of Art, Washington
Index of American Design
1943.8.8135 (SOCAL-mscl-doll-
151)

*Hooked Rug,* 1780
Rendered by H. Langden Brown,
c. 1937
watercolor, gouache, and graphite
0.419 x 0.680 m (16½ x 26¾ in)
National Gallery of Art, Washington
Index of American Design
1943.8.11228 (ILL-te-23)

*Perforated Tin Lantern,* late 18th
century or early 19th century
Rendered by Oscar Bluhme, 1940
watercolor, graphite, and gouache
0.511 x 0.375 m (20⅛ x 14¾ in)
National Gallery of Art, Washington
Index of American Design
1943.8.11388 (ILL-me-157)

*Quilt Block,* 1870
Rendered by Florence Truelson,
c. 1935/1942
watercolor and gouache
0.375 x 0.368 m (14¾ x 14½ in)
National Gallery of Art, Washington
Index of American Design
1943.8.219 (UTAH-te-48)

*Sampler,* 1813
Rendered by Alfred Walbeck,
c. 1938
watercolor, graphite, and gouache
0.324 x 0.349 m (12¾ x 13¾ in)
National Gallery of Art, Washington
Index of American Design
1943.8.15 (FLA-te-24)

*Sampler,* 1822
Rendered by Charlotte Angus,
c. 1937
watercolor, gouache, and graphite
0.381 x 0.508 m (15 x 20 in)
National Gallery of Art, Washington
Index of American Design
1943.8.23 (PA-te-8)

*Stenciled Chair,* 1829
Rendered by Lawrence Flynn, 1938
watercolor, colored pencil, and pen
and ink
0.381 x 0.278 m (15 x 10¹⁵⁄₁₆ in)
National Gallery of Art, Washington
Index of American Design
1943.8.4345 (CONN-fu-96a)

*Stoneware Crock,* c. 1860
Rendered by George Loughridge,
c. 1938
watercolor and graphite
0.451 x 0.380 m (17¾ x 14¹⁵⁄₁₆ in)
National Gallery of Art, Washington
Index of American Design
1943.8.7357 (NYC-cer-st-223)

*Weather Vane: Horse,*
late 18th century
Rendered by Isidore Sovensky,
c. 1937
watercolor and graphite
0.226 x 0.292 m (8⅞ x 11½ in)
National Gallery of Art, Washington
Index of American Design
1943.8.11224 (NYC-me-i-39)

*Weather Vane: Indian,*
early 19th century
Rendered by Rollington Campbell,
c. 1936
graphite
0.292 x 0.229 m (11½ x 9 in)
National Gallery of Art, Washington
Index of American Design
1943.8.11226 (NYC-me-i-56)

*Weather Vane: Rooster,*
late 18th century
Rendered by Salvatore Borrazzo, c.
1936
graphite
0.289 x 0.229 m (11⅜ x 9 in)
National Gallery of Art, Washington
Index of American Design
1943.8.11222 (NYC-me-i-89)

*Weather Vane: Squirrel,* c. 1797
Rendered by Mildred E. Bent,
c. 1935/1942
watercolor and graphite
0.248 x 0.357 m (9¾ x 14¹⁄₁₆ in)
National Gallery of Art, Washington
Index of American Design
1943.8.11225 (ME-me-5)

DEMCO